WALLPAPER

Clare Taylor

Shire Publications Ltd

CONTENTS

Printed in Great Britain by C. I. Thomas & Sons (Haverfordwest) Ltd, Press Buildings, Merlins Bridge, Haverfordwest, Dyfed SA61 1XF.

British Library Cataloguing in Publication Data: Taylor, Clare. Wallpaper. I. Title. 747.3. ISBN 0-7478-0140-1.

ACKNOWLEDGEMENTS
The author is grateful to the following for permission to reproduce wallpapers from their collections for the illustrations specified: Ancient High House, Stafford Borough Council, page 8 (top right and bottom); Birmingham Museum and Art Gallery, pages 9 and 17 (top right); Bourne Hall Museum, Epsom, page 4; Ferens Art Gallery, Hull City Museums and Art Galleries, cover and page 5; Ipswich Borough Museums and Galleries, page 7 (top left); Mr and Mrs A. G. Jarvis, page 8 (top left); Knebworth House (Arthur Pickett), page 32; Manchester City Art Galleries, pages 7 (top right and bottom), 17 (top left and bottom), 20 (bottom two), 23 (top right), 25 (top) and 28 (both); Silver Studio Collection, Middlesex Polytechnic, pages 22 (bottom), 23 (bottom) and 25 (bottom); Temple Newsam House, Leeds City Art Galleries, pages 2, 6 and 11; Towneley Hall Art Gallery and Museums, Burnley Borough Council, page 10 (both); Whitworth Art Gallery, University of Manchester, pages 1, 3, 12-16 (all), 18-19 (all), 20 (top), 21 (all), 22 (top), 23 (left), 24 (both), 26-7 (all) and 29.

Cover: *The production of block-printed and flocked wallpaper at a workshop in Hull, c.1842. The complete picture is shown on page 5: see its caption for details.*

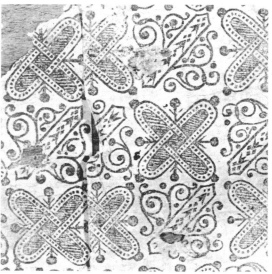

Left: *This diaper-pattern lining paper, block-printed in black ink, c.1640-50, was found lining an oak box in the collection of Temple Newsam House, Leeds. The pattern is related to motifs found in contemporary black-stitch needlework.*

Previous page: *The earliest known English wallpaper, which hung in the Master's Lodge of Christ's College, Cambridge. The lodge was built in 1509 and the paper is block-printed in black ink on the reverse of printed sheets which contain references to events of that year. The monogram (h) and goose are thought to relate to Hugo Goes, a blockmaker and printer from Beverley, Humberside. This reconstruction of the pattern was machine-printed by Horace Warner of Jeffrey and Company in 1911.*

A stag-hunting scene, block-printed in black ink and stencilled in yellow, red and green, late seventeenth century. It is possible that the landscape setting and narrative subject of this paper, now in the Whitworth Art Gallery, Manchester, were derived from imported Chinese wallpapers.

THE ORIGINS OF WALLPAPER: 1500-1690

Although many people hang wallpaper on their walls, it is only comparatively recently that wallpaper's history from its origins in the sixteenth century has begun to be studied and documented. The importance of wallpaper in the history of interior decoration is now being appreciated, as is its value as a reflector of changes in taste and fashion. Although early wallpapers took up the designs of materials already in use as wall coverings, wallpaper makers rapidly developed their own original designs, later employing well known designers and artists.

One of the problems of research into the history of wallpaper is the ephemeral nature of the material. The history of the industry is being pieced together from papers found hanging in their original settings (often only fragments, hidden by later decorative schemes), manufacturers' archives, illustrations of techniques and documentary sources.

It is difficult to establish when printed papers were first used as wall decorations in Britain. Few sixteenth-century and seventeenth-century papers have been discovered hanging in their original settings and this may be a reflection of the scarcity of their use, as well as of their ephemeral nature. There is evidence that some designs were used as borders or small friezes above the level of wood panelling. The earliest English wallpaper, printed with a pomegranate pattern and dated *c*.1509, was found in this position as well as pasted on to the plaster between sections of panelling. However, other papers, such as one of the late seventeenth century found at Alderman Fenwick's House in Newcastle upon Tyne, were pasted over all of a room's vertical surfaces.

The designs of sixteenth-century and seventeenth-century papers followed those found on the more costly wall coverings with which paper was intended to compete:

velvets, brocades, tapestries, leather hangings and painted or panelled surfaces. Heraldic designs displaying coats of arms imitated wall paintings and painted canvas or linen hangings. Narrative scenes, depicting events from outdoor life or mythology, were also used, inspired by contemporary tapestries and illustrations. Patterns from embroidery or needlework, in particular the floral motifs of black stitch executed on a white ground and the distinctive designs of flame stitch, in which each element is worked in a single graduated colour, are also found in wallpapers. Contemporary textiles also inspired wallpaper patterns, and some papers may have been produced by woodblock printers who also printed textiles.

Our knowledge of early wallpaper makers is scanty, but it is likely that the early

This floral pattern, block-printed in black ink on paper washed in buff, is related to a lace or needlework design. It was found in a first-floor room in The Shrubbery, Epsom, Surrey, pasted directly on to the lath and plaster, and partly overlaid by a paper printed with a pattern similar to the stag-hunting scene on page 3. Identical designs have been found at Alderman Fenwick's House, Newcastle upon Tyne, and at a house in Kingston upon Thames, Surrey.

papers were produced by a small number of printers who were already employed in other work, printing book illustrations and decorated papers, the latter for use as lining papers and bookend papers. Where their context is not known, the wallpapers which survive from the sixteenth and seventeenth centuries can be hard to distinguish from lining papers. In general the size of a pattern (called the repeat) and the complexity of the design indicate whether or not a paper was intended to be seen on the wall. A further clue is that, if several sheets survive, each printed with a different portion of the pattern, the complete repeat becomes visible only when the sheets are hung next to each other on the wall. These patterns differ from the small linear patterns favoured for lining papers intended to cover the interior of cupboards, chests or boxes.

The techniques used in the production of sixteenth-century papers were very simple. A large proportion of the surviving papers are printed in black ink from a woodblock on to individual sheets of paper. Neither the woodblock nor the paper was a standard size. By the end of the seventeenth century coloured papers were relatively common, produced by brushing watercolour on to the paper before printing, or adding colour through a stencil over the printed outline. This was not always done very carefully so colour often overran the edges of the design. The earliest colours used included red, green, blue, orange and yellow.

However, the quality of printing was still poor and the range of designs limited. It is possible that this restricted range was due to technical problems, but it is also likely that these papers were produced for a small, but expanding, middle-class market. By the 1690s printed papers had become an acceptable type of wall decoration among wealthy merchants in places as far apart as Epsom in Surrey and Newcastle upon Tyne. Wallpaper was not only preferable to a painted plaster finish but also provided a fashionable effect more cheaply than panelling or textiles. Nevertheless, wallpaper could not yet challenge the dominance of more costly wall coverings in the homes of the upper classes.

A wallpaper-printing workshop, Hull, c.1842. This view shows three stages in the production of block-printed wallpaper. The printer works in good light in front of the window, using a weighted wooden treadle to apply pressure to the block, which prints on to paper whose ground has already been coloured. When not in use, other blocks hang on the wall behind the flocking table, where a man is shaking cut flock through a mesh on to the prepared paper. To the right, paper which has been printed in several colours hangs up to dry before being cut to length and rolled up for dispatch. The only changes made to this technique in the nineteenth century were the use of continuous rolls of paper and the weighted treadle.

SOCIAL ACCEPTABILITY: 1690-1800

Printed papers were probably introduced into aristocratic homes in the first quarter of the eighteenth century as suitable decorations for servants' rooms. However, in the 1680s two developments took place which finally enabled paper hangings to compete with more expensive textile and leather hangings: individual sheets began to be joined together in groups of twelve to form a 'piece' or roll, enabling faster printing of more complex designs; and 'flocking', a technique already in use on cloth,

began to be applied to paper. The technique involved the application of adhesive to the paper either by brush through a stencil or by using a woodblock. Finely sifted, bleached and dyed wool shearings (a by-product of cloth manufacture) were blown or shaken through a sieve on to this surface. The problem of flock peeling off the ground was solved in the 1740s by varnishing the previously coloured paper before the adhesive was applied. Flocks could now compete with more costly materials both in

price and appearance. In the 1750s flocks ranged in price from 4 to 12 shillings a yard; even an elaborate high-quality design cost less than half the price of cut velvet. The method was particularly suitable for reproducing the formal damask patterns of this fabric as the flock produced a three-dimensional raised effect, the shiny varnished ground contrasting with the matt flock. The range of colours was extended from blue, green and red to include yellow, purple and brown. Flocks were also produced with a contrasting block-printed ground.

By the 1740s flocks had become widely popular in the reception rooms and best bedchambers of the aristocracy. The most popular designs survive in a number of different colourways, where the same design is printed up in different colour combinations. For example, a design of stylised flowers and foliage flocked in red was hung in the Privy Council's offices in London around 1735 and was also used at Christchurch Mansion, Ipswich, (in red on buff) and at Clandon Park, Surrey, (in green) at a similar date.

Flocks were considerably more durable than printed papers, which were cheaper and therefore used in the less public areas of great houses. Frequently the pattern of a flock was reduced in scale and block-printed (often in a different colourway) for use in a bedchamber. Attention was also given to the aspect of a room in selecting the paper's colour: there is clear evidence

Left: Formal design of stylised flowers, block-printed in two shades of green on a yellow ground, 1860s. Found in a lobby at Temple Newsam House, Leeds, but almost certainly also hung in an adjacent bedroom. The design is identical to the red flock paper hung in the Long Gallery in 1827.

Facing page: Eighteenth-century flocks. (Top left) Formal pattern of stylised flowers and foliage, red flock on buff ground, stamped with the Georgian Excise duty mark on the back, 1730-5; found on a dressing-room partition at Christchurch Mansion, Ipswich, where an identical pattern hangs in the state bedroom. (Top right) 'Lustre paper': sprigs of flowers and foliage flocked in red and green on a mica-dusted ground, stamped with the Georgian Excise duty mark, 'PAPER (?J8)', on the back, c.1740-50. The joints where the individual sheets have been pasted together are clearly visible. (Bottom) Floral pattern, red flock on pink ground, from Wythenshawe Hall, Manchester, late eighteenth century. Found behind bookcases installed in the library wing in 1813, this paper was probably hung when the room was built in the late 1790s.

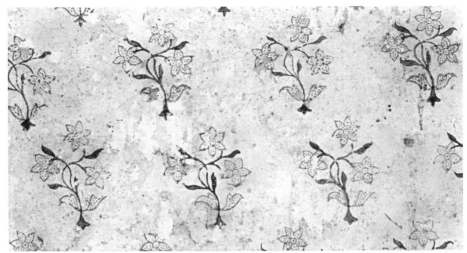

Above: *Simple two-colour sprig, block-printed in red and blue and stamped on the back with the Georgian Excise duty mark, 'PAPER J9', c.1760. From the closet of King Charles's Room, Aston Hall, Birmingham.*

that south-facing rooms were decorated in cool blues and greens, north-facing apartments in warmer reds, pinks and yellows. Blue, green and red (the last used extensively in picture galleries to set off the gilt frames) remained the most popular choices for reception rooms.

The further development of block-printed wallpapers was inhibited not only by the success of flocks but also by the difficulty of printing in more than one colour. By the 1750s experiments with distemper colours had enabled printed-paper manufacturers to extend their range. These gave matt opaque effects by mixing powder colour with a water-based (rather than oil-based) medium, usually glue or size. Pea green and a bluey-green colour called 'verditure' appear to have been particularly popular and are frequently mentioned in contemporary inventories of household goods and accounts. Papers printed with a single colour were often used with a border which followed the line of the room's architectural features. Sometimes contrasting in colour and flocked, silvered or gilded, the borders were printed with an architectural motif, scrolling or floral patterns.

Plain papers were also printed with *trompe l'oeil* frames, intended to make the viewer think they were real, into which prints of classical scenes taken from Old Masters could be pasted. These were used to create country-house 'print rooms' in a fashion which flourished briefly in the 1750s and 1760s, initiated by Horace Walpole in the parlour of his Middlesex villa, Strawberry Hill. Walpole's prints were supplied by a Frenchman, John Baptist Jackson. Jackson experimented in the early 1750s with chiaroscuro printing, using woodcuts to produce a three-dimensional effect by printing in light and dark tones with oil-based colours. How-

Facing page, top left: *Print-room paper, block-printed in grey, khaki, blue, white and black, c.1760. This design is one of three print-room papers which were hung at Doddington Hall, Lincolnshire, around 1760.*

Facing page, top right and bottom: *Gothic wall (top right) and ceiling (bottom) papers block-printed in brown, black and white on a grey ground and stamped on the back with the Georgian Excise duty mark, 'PAPER 3', c.1760. The figure panel was pasted directly on to the wattle and daub, framed by the ceiling paper pasted on to the timbers, on the staircase at the Ancient High House, Stafford.*

ever, his papers were not commercially successful and by 1755 he was out of business. Other makers were quick to produce papers ready-printed with both frame and print in a range of ground colours, such as those which survive from Doddington Hall, Lincolnshire.

Walpole seems to have been responsible for popularising another eighteenth-century wallpaper pattern, the Gothic paper which took its inspiration from architectural motifs. He used a paper printed with a Gothic fretwork pattern on the staircase at Strawberry Hill, and this type of design became popular for use in halls and on stairs, usually printed in bluey-greys on a cream ground.

Other fashions in wallpaper design were derived from textiles and paper hangings imported from the East. Small-scale floral designs copied from Indian chintzes were popular for use in closets and servants'

rooms in large houses and were also used to decorate more modest homes. Printed in one or two colours, by 1754 they cost between 4d and 1s 2d per yard. The cheapest designs were simple stripes, sprigs or checks.

Most expensive were the sets of hand-painted Chinese papers which the East India Company had begun to import in the last years of the seventeenth century. Confusingly referred to as 'China', 'Japan' or 'India' paper, they consisted of sets of between twenty-five and forty rolls painted in gouache (opaque watercolour paint) or tempera (powder colour mixed with organic gums) on pale-coloured grounds with a non-repeating pattern. This usually showed a landscape full of naturalistic detail of birds and plants or, more rarely, scenes of everyday life, or a combination of the two. Because they were expensive, around 14 shillings per sheet in the 1750s, they were

Simple leaf and sprig designs from Towneley Hall, Burnley, Lancashire. (Left) Black and white leaves and stems block-printed on a grey ground, 1765-75. (Right) Sprigs block-printed in blues on a buff ground, late eighteenth century. The 'pinhead' effect is achieved by the insertion of copper pins into the woodblock.

Chinese export paper, hand-painted on a blue-grey ground with garden scenes, hung in the Chinese Drawing Room at Temple Newsam House, Leeds, c.1827.

11

usually hung in small closets and bed-chambers in great houses. Painted to order, they could take more than a year to arrive but were nevertheless in great demand. English paper manufacturers produced their own imitations of Chinese papers, which nevertheless remain European in style and were made from entirely different types of paper, often using printed as well as painted motifs.

By the end of the eighteenth century the manufacture and sale of wallpaper had become separated from the trade of general printers. At the beginning of the century stationers and booksellers were the main retailers of wallpaper, with the occasional reference to a paper merchant producing a design as a special order. By the late 1750s upholsterers were dealing in wallpapers as part of their business supplying house furniture and soft furnishings. The majority of provincial dealers' stock was still supplied by manufacturers of paper hangings, paper stainers, in London at this date. By the 1770s these upholsterers had their own warehouses or shops attached to their

English chinoiserie design, printed from a metal plate and stencilled, stamped on the back with the Georgian Excise duty mark, 'PAPER J', c.1770. The motifs are borrowed from Chinese examples, although their arrangement is wholly European in inspiration.

works, which were promoted by elaborate trade cards, and were competing with paper stainers, who were by now becoming established in provincial towns. These firms sold papers in a wide price range and also arranged to hang wallpaper.

Contemporary illustrations indicate that by the mid eighteenth century printed sources of ornament as well as tracings of textile patterns were being used by the block cutter. Blockmaking was a highly skilled job, requiring the division of a design into its constituent colours and the manufacture and carving of a separate block to print each colour. Manufacturers kept their own blocks, and new designs were produced either as special commissions (later to be added to stock), perhaps designed by an architect, or in response to new fashions and probably devised by the block cutter.

Reliable attributions of surviving papers to specific firms are only possible when the paper can be identified in contemporary accounts. Evidence of the activities of the more successful firms, such as Thomas Bromwich, can be obtained in this way. The Bromwich family had probably been printers at the end of the seventeenth century. By about 1740 Thomas was in business as a leather gilder, also making paper hangings and papier-mâché, on Ludgate Hill in London. Although Bromwich died in 1787, the business carried on until 1853. His was one of the workshops linked to the early use of distemper colour in block printing and Bromwich supplied Horace Walpole with paper for Strawberry Hill in 1754.

As wallpaper became more popular during the eighteenth century it became an obvious new source of taxation revenue: in 1712 the duty on plain paper was extended to painted, printed or stained hangings, which were taxed at 1d per square yard. In 1714 the tax was raised and each sheet in a piece or roll, made up of twelve sheets, was required to be stamped. A licence fee of 4 guineas was imposed on paper stainers, and duties and fees were raised again in 1787 and 1809. Duty was also imposed on imported papers from 1773 and from 1792 on Chinese paper.

Machine printing on four machines in a wallpaper factory, 1880. The largest machine printed in up to twelve colours.

WALLPAPER FOR ALL: 1800-90

The wallpaper industry was rather slow to meet the challenge of mechanisation which the nineteenth century brought to traditional industries. In part this was due to lack of technical innovation, as well as restrictions placed on production by the Excise Office.

In 1799 a Frenchman, Louis Robert, produced a model of a machine which could make continuous rolls of paper. This process was perfected by the Foudrinier brothers, working in England, and by 1806 rolls of paper were in production. However, the Excise Office did not allow these rolls to be used for wallpaper printing until 1830, presumably fearful of the effect it would have on the income from the duty on each piece. Innovations in printing methods were therefore not developed in Britain until the 1830s.

The main method of wallpaper printing at the beginning of the nineteenth century continued to be the woodblock, although A. L. Eckhardt, a wallpaper manufacturer working in Chelsea, had produced papers printed from engraved copper plates as early as 1792. In the 1830s experiments were made with engraved copper cylinders as used in calico printing, and in 1839 the firm of Potter and Ross, of Darwen, Lancashire, patented a steam-powered machine which used engraved metal rollers. This was later refined by using wooden rollers, where the pattern to be printed was left standing in relief, imitating the raised surface of woodblocks. Paper was fed around the rotating drum of this 'surface printing machine' and was printed as it passed over each roller in turn. Different colours and sections of the pattern could be printed at the same time as each roller had a separate colour trough. This machine produced much clearer prints than those printed from metal rollers, although in contrast to block-printed designs the early machine product used much thinner colours, a more restricted colour range and smaller repeats, because of the roll's diameter.

The repeal of the tax on a piece or roll of wallpaper in 1836 coincided with the development of machine printing, which by 1850 could print in up to eight colours.

Aniline dyes obtained from coal tar also extended the colour range to include the bright mauves, reds and blues so characteristic of mid nineteenth-century designs.

Although block printing continued in use right through the century, especially for more luxurious ranges, machine printing had an enormous impact on the industry. In 1834 1.05 million yards (960,000 metres) of paper were produced, but by 1860 this had risen to 9 million yards (8.2 million metres) and it could be as cheap to paper a room as to whitewash or stencil. Tenants and owners of homes in the expanding cities were a major new market. Polluted air, oil (and later gas) lighting and coal fires made frequent decoration a necessity which, together with the desire for a cheap and quick change of decoration in tenanted accommodation, contributed to the demand for wallpaper.

By the end of the eighteenth century the dominance of flocks as fashionable wall coverings was being successfully challenged by the products of French firms. Zuber et Compagnie perfected delicate shaded backgrounds on which designs of flowers, *trompe l'oeil* lace, ribbons and swagged silk were printed. The French also produced luxurious 'panoramic' decorations which consisted of up to thirty lengths which when joined formed a continuous scene around the wall. Subjects designed and printed by Zuber et Compagnie and other firms, such as Dufour et Compagnie, included mythological scenes and exotic landscapes. On a more modest scale, the French also popularised the 'pilaster' decoration, in which vertical and horizontal wallpaper borders were arranged around medallions printed with *trompe l'oeil* frames containing a figure or a bouquet of naturalistic flowers.

Elaborate, three-dimensional patterns were regarded with disdain by designers such as the architect A. W. N. Pugin. His own designs used two-dimensional motifs taken from medieval architecture and heraldry, printed in a restricted range of colours. Papers such as these contrasted sharply with those produced by the more conservative manufacturers, in particular papers designed for the mass market. English manufacturers bought and copied

Early machine print: a small-scale ivy trellis design produced by C. and G. Potter and Sons in the 1840s.

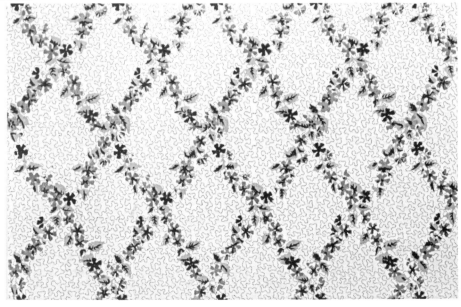

14

Panoramic decoration: 'The Reconciliation of Venus and Psyche' from 'Cupid and Psyche',
printed in greys from woodblocks. Issued by Dufour et Compagnie in 1816, the complete series
consisted of 26 panels forming twelve scenes and used over a thousand blocks.

French designs, and patterns imitating swagged drapery, rococo scrollwork and overblown roses were amongst the papers exhibited at the Great Exhibition in 1851. Pictorial papers were also shown, illustrating popular pastimes and contemporary events.

The firm of Jeffrey and Company, established in Islington around 1835, led British manufacturers in improvements in design quality. From the late 1860s the company was run by Metford Warner, who pioneered the recruitment of well known artists and architects to design wallpapers for his firm.

British wallpaper manufacturers at the Great Exhibition: block-printed pilaster decoration exhibited by Townsend, Parker and Company.

Above left: *A. W. N. Pugin (1812-52): design of national emblems within a trellis, colour print from woodblocks with flock, printed for the Houses of Parliament, c.1848-50.*

Above right: *Fleurs-de-lis printed in purple and pink on an embossed moiré background flocked in khaki, c.1858. This paper was hung in King Charles's Room and its closet for the visit of Queen Victoria to Aston Hall, Birmingham, in 1858, when she opened the house to the public.*

Their names were a good advertisement for Jeffrey and Company, and the improved quality of wallpaper patterns produced by designers for this and other firms helped to raise the status of the industry, which was admitted to the Fine Arts Exhibition at the Albert Hall for the first time in 1873. By the 1880s Jeffreys had an impressive list of prominent designers, including the designer and book illustrator Walter Crane, the painter Charles Eastlake and the craftsman and poet William Morris. Morris had turned to Jeffreys for help in 1864 when his experiments in printing wallpapers in transparent colours from zinc etched plates failed. His deceptively simple two-dimensional designs of naturalistic flowers and foliage printed in bright clear colours were an entirely new idea in wallpaper design. Walter Crane also used motifs and

Right: *British wallpaper manufacturers at the Great Exhibition: chiaroscuro panel after a painting by Murillo in the Dulwich Art Gallery exhibited by Jeffrey, Allen and Company.*

17

themes from nature in his designs. He attached symbolic meanings to his complex, richly coloured patterns, which featured exotic animals, birds, figures and even text.

Although the majority of Jeffrey and Company's designs were block-printed by hand and therefore expensive, some, such as a series of two-colour staircase papers designed by the architect Lewis F. Day, were machine-printed and sold quite cheaply. The firm's designs were also widely publicised in the pages of the many new magazines and books on decorating the home which appeared from the 1860s onwards.

Left: Lewis F. Day (1845-1910): 'Henri II', filling and border, two-colour machine print by Jeffrey and Company, c.1889; issued in a pattern book of 112 borders, friezes, fillings and dados, advertised as 'low-price wallpapers for staircase decoration designed by Lewis F. Day'.

Below: Drapery frieze, colour print from woodblocks, c.1860. Papers such as these imitated the skills of French manufacturers in printing three-dimensional effects.

Cabbage roses and rococo scrolls: colour print from woodblocks by Woollams and Company, c.1860.

Writers on home decoration exerted an enormous influence on wallpaper fashions in the latter half of the century. Certain designs were advocated for particular rooms: papers with marble, tile or wood patterns, imitating expensive hard-wearing surfaces, were recommended for halls, passages and stairs. They were particularly suitable for use on the dado or lower portion of the wall, usually up to 4 feet (1.2 metres) above the skirting. From the 1880s different wallpapers were used for the dado,

Left: *Floral dado, colour print from woodblocks by Jeffrey and Company, 1880.*

Below: *Walter Crane (1845-1915): (left) 'Macaw', 1908; (right) 'Peacocks and Amorini', 1878; both colour prints from woodblocks by Jeffrey and Company. The exotic birds and animals in these designs are typical of Crane's richly patterned papers. 'Peacocks and Amorini' was produced with a frieze and dado to complement this filling design.*

Designs by William Morris (1834-96), colour prints from woodblocks by Jeffrey and Company: (above left) 'Daisy', 1864; (above right) 'Acanthus', 1875; (below left) 'Pimpernel', 1876; (below right) 'Hammersmith', 1890. These designs illustrate the development of Morris's style in wallpaper design, from the simple motifs of 'Daisy', derived from an illuminated manuscript, to the tangled curving foliage of 'Acanthus' and the symmetrical and diagonal patterns of 'Pimpernel' and 'Hammersmith' respectively.

the 'filling' (the central part of the wall between the dado and the picture rail) and the frieze (between the picture rail and the cornice). Manufacturers promoted 'complete decorations' with different yet complementary designs for each section, borders and even ceiling papers. These schemes were particularly suited to lofty public buildings and hallways, where they created the illusion of a lower ceiling and gave added interest to large expanses of wall.

Flocks remained popular for the more formal rooms in the home; their durability and finish were suitable for rooms heated by coal fires and lit by oil or gas. Paler colours were recommended for bedrooms in patterns imitating silk moiré or satinette (the latter having a lustrous finish imitating silk damask, achieved by adding powdered mica to the mix), as well as the ever popular floral chintzes. Towards the end of the century special papers and friezes were printed for children's nurseries by designers such as Walter Crane, whose first design for Jeffrey and Company ('The Queen of Hearts', 1875) was derived from his book illustrations.

The wallpaper industry continued to develop new materials and print techniques during the second half of the nineteenth century. 'Sanitary' papers, printed by engraved copper rollers, which produced a smooth surface, using transparent oil-based colours, could be varnished to give a spongeable finish. They were first produced by the Manchester firm of Heywood,

Above and right: Tile papers: (above) colour machine print by John Stather and Sons Limited, c.1890; (right) sanitary wallpaper of stylised tulips on an imitation tile ground, designed by Harry Napper (1860-1940) at the Silver Studio, 1898; such designs were popular for use on dados and in bathrooms.

Left and above: 'Sanitary' wallpapers: (left) decoration for halls by Dugdale, Poole and Company, 1880-90; (above) detail of a dado designed by Christopher Dresser (1834-1904) for Lightbown, Aspinall and Company, c.1880.

Below: *Japanese-inspired design for a wallpaper by the Silver Studio, 1899.*

Above: *Pictorial paper, probably produced by Heywood, Higginbottom and Smith, c.1880: roller skating.*

Higginbottom and Smith in 1871, and the grainy effects produced by intaglio printing made them particularly suited to fine shaded designs. A wide range of embossed papers, which used heated metal rollers to produce raised designs, came on the market in the 1880s. These included Lincrusta Walton (patented in 1877) and the lighter in weight Anaglypta (invented in 1887), which were used extensively on dados, as when painted they produced a very durable finish.

Left: *'Golden Jubilee' design, colour print from woodblocks, 1887. One of many wallpapers produced to celebrate Queen Victoria's Golden Jubilee, this elaborate decoration consisting of a frieze, filling and dado was presumably intended for use in a public building rather than in the home.*

24

Pictorial paper, probably produced by Heywood, Higginbottom and Smith, c.1880: bicycling.

This design for a wallpaper frieze was probably executed by John Illingworth Kay (1870-1950) at the Silver Studio in 1893. The wallpaper manufacturer Charles Knowles bought a modified version without the figures.

Nursery frieze, sanitary print, probably designed by Will Owen (1869-1957) for Lightbown, Aspinall and Company, c.1920.

William Shand Kydd (1864-1936): 'Roma' frieze, colour print from woodblock and stencilling on Japanese grasspaper, c.1900.

Illustration of an interior with cut-out decorations used both as a frieze and to frame panels of wallpaper, c.1915.

THE TWENTIETH CENTURY

By the end of the nineteenth century a great range of wallpapers was available, varying widely in price, printing methods and style of design, and most homes contained some wallpaper. In 1899 some of the best known wallpaper-manufacturing firms amalgamated to form the Wallpaper Manufacturers Limited (WPM). The purpose of the company was to give financial support to smaller firms who were still printing by hand from woodblocks and to protect manufacturers from foreign competition. The WPM rapidly achieved a near monopoly of wallpaper production, as well as increasing the range of papers available at the cheaper end of the market.

Stylistic attention was focused on the frieze. 'Crown' decorations, which had been popularised at the end of the nineteenth century, consisted of a vertical design in the filling, often a flowering tree whose blossom filled the area of the frieze. By 1900 pattern was increasingly concentrated in the frieze alone, which could be between 21 inches and 4 feet (53-122 cm) deep, and available in embossed, printed or stencilled paper. Subject matter included landscapes, classical and maritime scenes and scrolling Art Nouveau inspired flowers. William Shand Kydd (1864-1938), who stencilled and block-printed friezes and accompanying fillings and borders in the 1900s and 1920s, was well known for his avant-garde friezes, produced for wealthier customers.

Friezes were also among the many wallpapers designed by the Silver Studio, a commercial decorative arts design practice founded by Arthur Silver (1853-96) in 1880. The firm's output included wallpapers in a wide range of traditional and contemporary styles which sold to manufacturers including Jeffrey and Company,

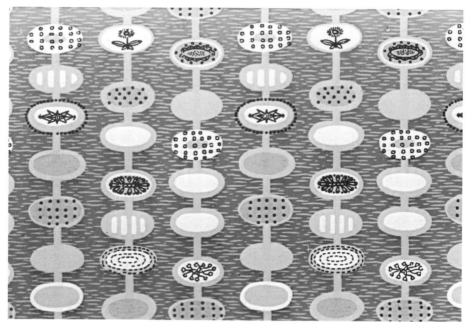

Above and below: *Colour screen prints by John Line and Sons Limited: (above) 'Provence',
designed by Lucienne Day for 'Limited Editions 1951'; (below) 'Insulin', design by William J.
Odell based on a crystalline structure for the Festival of Britain, 1951.*

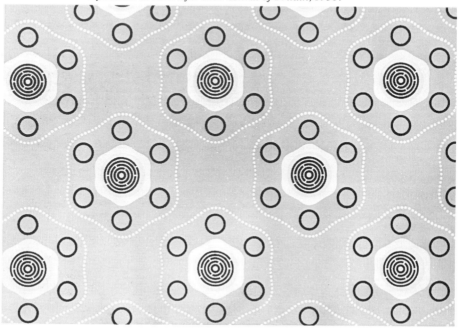

Lightbown, Aspinall and Company and Woollams and Company.

After the First World War friezes gave way to cut-out appliqué borders and corners in floral patterns, including (by the 1920s) geometric designs showing the influence of Jazz Age decorative art. These were accompanied by pale, textured filling papers. The more conservative householder chose papers inspired by 'Old English' textiles and leather hangings to complement neo-Tudor designs in architecture and furniture. Patterns from historic printed papers were also reproduced, a trend which has continued and grown into the 1990s. Embossed papers such as Lincrusta and Anaglypta continued to be popular, sometimes used with papers imitating wood panelling.

By the late 1920s wallpaper had virtually disappeared from avant-garde interiors and, although Edward Bawden's wallpaper designs produced in the 1930s enjoyed some popularity, it was not until the 1950s that wallpapers designed by well known artists and designers became part of the fashionable interior once more.

In 1950 the Council for Industrial Design issued a folio of contemporary designs in wallpaper including papers produced by well known wallpaper companies like Sandersons, Coles, John Line and Shand Kydd. In the following year John Line issued 'Limited Edition 1951', the first screen-printed British wallpapers, which included work by the company's own and well known freelance designers. Designs based on crystalline structure and organic cross-sections revealed by the new technique of microphotography were also exhibited by Line at the Festival of Britain in the same year.

The WPM followed Line's lead, introducing its own screen prints in 1955 as the Palladio range, many designed by young artists. The Palladio series continued in the 1960s and by 1968 included vinyls, produced by bonding a PVC coating on to paper. These gave the washable finish which 'sanitaries' had tried to achieve. New printing techniques such as photogravure were also applied to wallpaper in the 1960s and used by Shand Kydd in their Focus series to produce realistic imitations

'Apollo', colour screen print designed by John Wilkinson for Arthur Sanderson and Sons' 'Palladio 9' collection, c.1969-70.

29

of contemporary textiles.

Since the 1970s there has been an enormous boom in the use of wallpaper, in particular as part of co-ordinated ranges of textiles, papers, borders and accessories for the home. These are now marketed by firms ranging from designer-controlled concerns to chain stores. One of the strongest themes in design has been the revival of original textile and wallpaper patterns, known as 'document' designs, thereby continuing a tradition begun in the sixteenth century.

FINDING AND REMOVING OLD WALLPAPER

Few rooms, other than those in country houses or important public buildings, are likely to retain immediately obvious traces of their original decoration. However, rebuilding or redecoration often provides an opportunity to search for evidence of earlier schemes.

Because of the expense of stripping a wall of paper before hanging a new design, layers of paper may sometimes survive, particularly in nineteenth-century properties which have been tenanted. More costly methods of covering over an earlier paper include boarding and linen or canvas stretched over battens. If a paper was to be covered over during alterations it was rarely stripped: fragments are therefore often found behind partition walls or chimneypieces (where small fire surrounds were often replaced by larger designs), underneath a plate or picture rail and behind radiators or electric fittings. If the height of a skirting board has been raised and if a door or window frame has been enlarged the woodwork may conceal evidence of wallpaper. Wood panelling, disused shutters and semi-fitted furniture such as bookcases or mirrors may well conceal traces. A jibdoor may also be a useful starting point since it may not have been stripped as carefully as the surrounding wall. Even floorboards may conceal scraps of paper.

The exact location of any finds should be recorded on a plan of the room, and a photograph or tracing and a description made of the fragments. The size of the piece should also be related to the repeat and paper width. Design and printing method are the most obvious clues to dating, together with details of any stamps or registration numbers. If it is decided to remove the wallpaper, it is very important to seek the help of a specialist paper conservator, who can also help to identify the type of paper on which the design is printed. Secondary sources such as pictures or photographs of the interior and account books, diaries or descriptions relating to the building may help to establish when a room was redecorated. Local libraries, museums and record offices may help in tracing these.

FURTHER READING

Banham, J. *William Morris Wallpapers and Victorian Wallpaper Design*. Whitworth Art Gallery, Manchester, 1984.

— *A Decorative Art: Nineteenth Century Wallpapers in the Whitworth Art Gallery*. Whitworth Art Gallery, Manchester, 1985.

Clark, F. *William Morris Wallpapers and Chintzes*. Academy Editions, 1973.

Entwisle, E. A. *The Book of Wallpaper*. Arthur Barker, 1954.

— *A Literary History of Wallpaper*. B. T. Batsford, 1960.

— *Wallpapers of the Victorian Era*. Frank Lewis, Leigh-on-Sea, 1964.

— *French Scenic Wallpapers*. Frank Lewis, Leigh-on-Sea, 1972.

Greysmith, B. *Wallpaper*. Studio Vista, 1976.

Hamilton, J. *An Introduction to Wallpaper*. HMSO, 1983.

Hamilton, J., and Oman, C. C. *Wallpapers: A History and Illustrated Catalogue to the Collection of the Victoria and Albert Museum*. Sotheby Publications, 1982.

Lynn, C. *Wallpaper in America*. W. W. Norton, New York, 1980.

Schoeser, M. *Fabrics and Wallpapers — Twentieth Century Designs.* Bell and Hyman, 1986.

Sugden, A. V., and Edmundson, J. L. *Potters of Darwen 1839-1939.* G. Falkner and Sons, Manchester, 1939.

— *A History of English Wallpaper 1509-1914.* B. T. Batsford, 1926.

Teynac, F.; Nolot, P.; and Vivian, J. D. *Wallpaper: A History.* Thames and Hudson, 1982.

Turner, M. *A London Design Studio 1880-1963: The Silver Studio Collection.* Lund Humphries and Middlesex Polytechnic, 1980.

Turner, M., *et al. Art Nouveau Designs from the Silver Studio Collection, 1985-1910.* Middlesex Polytechnic, 1986.

Turner, M., Pinney, M., and Hoskins, L. *A Popular Art: British Wallpapers 1930-1960.* Middlesex Polytechnic, 1989.

Wells-Cole, A. *Historic Paper Hangings from Temple Newsam and Other English Houses.* Leeds City Art Galleries, 1983.

Whitworth Art Gallery. *Historic Wallpapers in the Whitworth Art Gallery.* Whitworth Art Gallery, Manchester, 1972.

Woods, C. (editor). *Sanderson 1860-1985.* A. Sanderson and Sons, 1985.

— *The Magic Influence of Mr Kydd in Blocked and Stencilled Wallpapers 1900-25.* Whitworth Art Gallery, Manchester, 1989.

PLACES TO VISIT

MUSEUMS

The collections listed below are in many cases not on permanent display but are usually available for study by prior appointment and are shown in occasional temporary exhibitions, details of which can be obtained from the institutions concerned.

The Design Archive, Arthur Sanderson and Sons Limited, 100 Acres, Oxford Road, Uxbridge, Middlesex UB8 1HY. Telephone: 0895 38244. Samples, designs, pattern books and records of the firm from 1860 to the present day.

Manchester City Art Gallery, Mosley Street, Manchester M2 3JL. Telephone: 061-236 5244. Samples and pattern books from the eighteenth century to the twentieth.

The Silver Studio Collection, Middlesex Polytechnic, Bounds Green Road, London N11 2NQ. Telephone: 081-368 1299 extension 7339. Designs, trials, catalogues and records of this London design studio which was active from 1880 to 1963.

Temple Newsam House, Leeds, West Yorkshire LS15 0AE. Telephone: 0532 647321 or 641358. Collection of provenanced papers dating from the seventeenth century to the nineteenth. Chinese scenic paper and reproductions of document papers hung in the house, and an exhibition of historic papers.

Victoria and Albert Museum, Cromwell Road, South Kensington, London SW7 2RL. Telephone: 071-938 8500. The national collection, including samples, designs and pattern books from the sixteenth century to the present day.

Whitworth Art Gallery, University of Manchester, Oxford Road, Manchester M15 6ER. Telephone: 061-273 4865. Samples, designs and pattern books from the seventeenth century to the present day.

COUNTRY HOUSES

The following is a selection of houses open to the public where one or more historic papers remain *in situ.* Visitors are advised to check in advance whether the relevant rooms are open.

Charlecote Park, Wellesbourne, Warwick CV35 9ER. Telephone: 0789 840277. National Trust. 1830s Elizabethan Revival papers.

Hand-painted eighteenth-century Chinese wallpaper in the Falkland Room at Knebworth House, Hertfordshire.

Chatsworth, Bakewell, Derbyshire DE4 1PP. Telephone: 0246 582204. Chinese scenic papers.

Christchurch Mansion, Christchurch Park, Ipswich, Suffolk. Telephone: 0473 213761 or 253246. Early eighteenth-century flock papers.

Clandon Park, West Clandon, Guildford, Surrey GU4 7RQ. Telephone: 0483 222482. National Trust. Eighteenth-century flock and printed papers.

Cragside House, Rothbury, Morpeth, Northumberland NE65 7PX. Telephone: 0669 20333. National Trust. Late nineteenth-century papers, including some by William Morris.

Doddington Hall, Doddington, Lincoln. Telephone: 0522 694308. Early nineteenth-century French scenic paper and late eighteenth-century English papers.

Erddig, near Wrexham, Clwyd LL13 0YT. Telephone: 0978 355314. National Trust. Chinese scenic papers.

Knebworth House, Knebworth, Hertfordshire SG3 6PY. Telephone: 0438 812661. Chinese scenic papers.

Nostell Priory, Nostell, near Wakefield, West Yorkshire WF4 1QE. Telephone: 0924 863892. National Trust. Chinese scenic papers.

Penrhyn Castle, Bangor, Gwynedd LL57 4HN. Telephone: 0248 353084. National Trust. Chinese scenic papers.

Saltram, Plympton, Plymouth, Devon PL7 3UH. Telephone: 0752 336546. National Trust. Chinese scenic papers.

Speke Hall, The Walk, Speke, Liverpool L24 1XD. Telephone: 051-427 7231. National Trust. William Morris papers.

Standen, near East Grinstead, West Sussex RH19 4NE. Telephone: 0342 23029. National Trust. William Morris papers.

Wightwick Manor, Wolverhampton, West Midlands WV6 8EE. Telephone: 0902 761108. National Trust. William Morris papers.